INDIA

Anita Ganeri and Rachel Wright

FRANKLIN WATTS

This symbol appears on some pages throughout this book. It indicates that adult supervision is advisable for that activity.

This edition 2007

Franklin Watts
338 Euston Road
London NW1 3BH

Franklin Watts Australia
Hachette Children's Books
Level 17/207 Kent Street
Sydney, NSW 2000

Editor: Hazel Poole
Designer: Sally Boothroyd
Commissioned photography: Peter Millard
Artwork: John Shackell
Picture research: Veneta Bullen

A CIP catalogue record for this book is available from the British Library.

ISBN-13: 978 0 7496 7330 7

Printed in China

Franklin Watts is a division of Hachette Children's Books.

CONTENTS

Introducing India

NAMASTE!

Hello and welcome to India! Before you begin your journey, here are a few facts and figures about India to help you on your way.

THE INDIAN FLAG

The Indian flag has three horizontal stripes in orange, white and green. There is a dark blue wheel in the middle of the white stripe. Each part of the flag has a special meaning. The orange stripe represents the Hindus of India, the green stripe the Muslims, and the white stripe the hope that the two can live in peace. The wheel is an ancient Buddhist symbol. It stands for peaceful change. The flag was adopted in 1947, when India gained its independence from the British (see pages 28–29).

INDIA IN THE WORLD

India is the largest country in South Asia and the seventh biggest country in the world. It is roughly diamond-shaped and covers an area of some 3,288,000 square kilometres. This includes the tiny Andaman and Nicobar Islands and the Lakshadweep Islands in the Indian Ocean. There is coastline down two sides of the country. On land, India has borders with Pakistan, Nepal, China, Bhutan, Bangladesh and Myanmar. Delhi is the capital of India. It is divided into two parts – the ancient city of Old Delhi, and the modern city of New Delhi. Delhi is the third largest city in India, after Calcutta and Mumbai (Bombay).

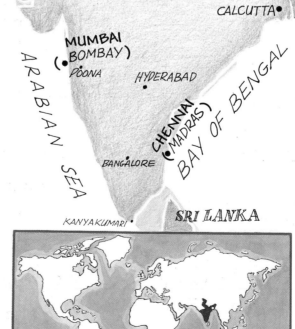

India is a republic and the world's largest democracy (a country whose government is elected by the people). It is made up of 25 states, and seven union territories (such as islands and large cities). The president is head of state, and the prime minister head of the government. The government buildings are in New Delhi.

NATIONAL SYMBOLS

The peacock is the national bird of India. But the national emblem of India is the four-lion capital (sculpture) of King Ashoka. It dates from the 3rd century BC. It originally stood on top of a tall pillar, which Ashoka had built in honour of the Buddha. Each part of the capital symbolises the teachings of the Buddha. Below the capital there is a motto in Sanskrit, the ancient language of India. It says, "Truth alone triumphs".

The Indian national anthem is *Jana-gana-mana* which means "Thou art the ruler of the minds of all people". It was composed by the poet Rabindranath Tagore, who won the Nobel Prize for Literature in 1913.

MONEY AND STAMPS

The Indian currency is called the *rupee*, written as R or Rs. One *rupee* is divided into 100 *paisa* (p). Coins and bank notes show the lion capital emblem, and the Hindi name for India, *Bharat*. The notes give their value in several different Indian scripts (see below). The word *Bharat* also appears on Indian stamps.

THE LANGUAGES OF INDIA

The words in the "Say it in" boxes throughout this book are in Hindi, India's main language. But India has 15 official languages, including English, and hundreds of local dialects. Different languages use different alphabets. Hindi is written in the Devanagri alphabet. The letters in a word are linked by a line running across the top.

Say it in Hindi

नमस्ते *namasstay* – hello

भारत *bharat* – India

भारती *bhaartee* – Indian

पैसा *paysaa* – money

हाँ *haan* – yes

नहीं *naheen* – no

Around India

India is such a huge country, and there are so many places to visit and amazing sights to see, that you'll be spoilt for choice. There are high mountains, a sandy desert and palm-fringed beaches. There are also many ancient buildings, temples and monuments to explore.

THE RED FORT

The Red Fort, or *Lal Qila*, in Delhi was built by Shah Jahan, in 1638. The fort has huge, red sandstone walls over 30 metres high in places. You can have a guided tour of the buildings inside the fort, or enjoy a sound and light show in the evening.

INDIAN GEOGRAPHY

The map on the right shows the main geographical regions of India and just a few of the many places well worth a visit. The Indian landscape is very varied. In the north, there are the great, snow-capped peaks of the Himalayas, the highest mountains in the world. In the west lies the dry, sandy Thar Desert. The River Ganges flows across a vast plain on its journey from the Himalayas to the Bay of Bengal. This is a very fertile area for crops. There is a tropical rainforest in the south.

TAJ MAHAL

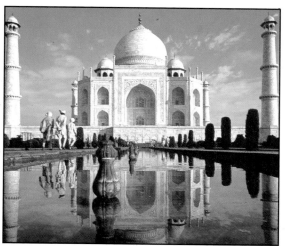

The Taj Mahal overlooks the River Yamuna in Agra. It was also built by the Mughal Emperor, Shah Jahan, in memory of his dead wife, Mumtaz. Shah Jahan wanted it to be the most beautiful building ever seen. He hired architects and craftsmen from all over the world. Work began in 1632 and lasted for 20 years. The Taj Mahal is built of white marble, inlaid with semi-precious stones.

MONSOON

Most of India has three seasons – hot, wet and cool. The wet season is caused by the monsoon winds which blow in off the Indian Ocean, bringing the rain needed for crops. The hot season begins in February. The wet season begins with the arrival of the monsoon in June. The cool season begins in October. This is the best time of year to visit India.

SHORE TEMPLES

Beautiful stone temples line the shore at Mahabalipuram, near Chennai (Madras) in South India. They were built in the 7th century AD and are dedicated to the Hindu gods, Vishnu and Shiva. South India is famous for its temples. Some have very brightly painted gateways.

THE GOLDEN TEMPLE

The Golden Temple in Amritsar is the holiest shrine of the Sikh religion. The temple has been destroyed and rebuilt several times. In 1802, it was given a copper roof which gleams golden in the sun. The temple is surrounded by a lake.

THE WIND PALACE

The Wind Palace in Jaipur is really a screen made of red sandstone, with rows of carved windows and balconies. It was built in 1799. At that time, the ladies of the royal court could sit behind the screen and watch the world go by, without being seen themselves.

Say it in Hindi

पहाड़ *pahaar* – mountain

नदी *nadee* – river

बरसात *barsaat* – monsoon, wet season

सूरज *sooraj* – sun

महल *mahal* – palace

Food and Drink

There are Indian restaurants all over the world and Indian food has become very popular. Indian dishes are very tasty. They can also be very hot and spicy, so choose carefully!

FOOD AROUND INDIA

In India, what you eat depends on where you live and on your religious beliefs. Many Hindus are vegetarians – they do not believe in killing things to eat. Some do eat chicken, and fish if they live along the coast, but Hindus never eat beef. They consider cows to be sacred animals. Muslims eat chicken (tandoori chicken is a famous Muslim dish) and lamb, but they will not eat pork.

A HINDU MEAL

A typical Hindu, vegetarian meal consists of several small dishes of spicy vegetables, *dhal* (like thick lentil soup), pickles, poppadums and rice or bread. More rice is grown in the south so more is eaten there. Wheat is grown in North India and made into different types of flat bread, such as *chapattis* and *naans*. Yoghurt *(dahi)* is another important part of a meal. It helps to cool down your mouth if you have eaten something fiery!

People eat off metal trays, called *thalis*, with each dish in a small metal bowl, or off banana leaves. They eat with their fingers. But they only use their right hands because their left hands are thought to be unclean.

After a meal, people chew *paan* to help them digest their food. This is a mixture of betel nut, spices and lime paste wrapped up in a triangular betel nut. It turns your teeth red if you eat too much!

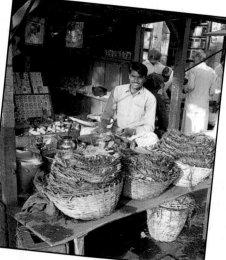

GOING SHOPPING

Indian people shop for fresh vegetables, fruit and other ingredients at the market. There are large indoor markets in the big towns and cities, and small local markets or rows of wayside stalls in the villages. There are also market stalls piled high with colourful spices, flowers for offering at the temple, and tasty takeaway snacks.

AND, TO DRINK

With a meal, people usually drink water or a refreshing yoghurt drink, called *lassi*. This can be sweet (flavoured with sugar) or sour (flavoured with salt). But the favourite Indian drink is hot, sweet, milky tea. After all, more tea is grown in India than anywhere else!

If you have a sweet tooth, there are plenty of Indian sweets to choose from. Some are sticky and syrupy, such as *jalebi* or *gulab jamun*. Others are made from milk or cream cheese, such as *rasgullas* or *sandesh*. Sweets are often given as gifts on special occasions, such as weddings, or as thank-you presents.

Shopping list

दूध	*doodh*	– milk
मिर्च	*mirch*	– chilli pepper
रोटी	*rotee*	– bread (chapatti)
आलू	*aloo*	– potato
गोभी	*gobee*	– cauliflower
आम	*aam*	– mango
चावल	*chaawal*	– rice
सब्ज़ी	*sabzee*	– vegetables

Curry and Spice

Indian cooks like to season their foods with a variety of spices. Some of these spices have a very delicate flavour. Others are so red-hot they can make your eyes water! The measurements of the spices listed in the recipe below will give you a very mild curry.

Potato and Cauliflower Curry is especially tasty when served with rice, chapattis or any other type of Indian bread. If you decide to serve bread, you can use it to scoop up your curry.

To feed two hungry people . . .

YOU WILL NEED:

LARGE, HEAVY SAUCEPAN

MEDIUM-SIZED SAUCEPAN

5 TABLESPOONS OF COOKING OIL

SMALL BOWL

SIEVE

120ml. WATER

SERVING DISH

LONG HANDLED WOODEN SPOON

1 MEDIUM-SIZED CAULIFLOWER

2 MEDIUM-SIZED POTATOES

CUTTING BOARD

SHARP KNIFE

A HANDFUL OF FRESH CORIANDER OR PARSLEY

2 HEAPED TEASPOONS OF TOMATO PURÉE

1 TEASPOON OF GARAM MASALA

½ TEASPOON OF CUMIN SEEDS

¼ TEASPOON OF CHILLI POWDER

1 TEASPOON OF TURMERIC POWDER

1 TEASPOON OF SALT

½ TEASPOON OF BLACK MUSTARD SEEDS

1. Wash and peel the potatoes and cut them into 2.5 cm cubes.

2. Partly fill the medium-sized saucepan with water. Put the pan on the ring and turn the heat to high. When the water boils, carefully add the potatoes and cook them for five minutes.

3. While the potatoes are cooking, chop the cauliflower into small florets and throw away any thick stalks. When the potatoes are ready, leave them to drain in the sieve.

4. Heat the oil in the large saucepan over a medium heat.

5. Mix the chilli powder, garam masala, cumin seeds, salt, turmeric powder and black mustard seeds in the bowl.

6. Tip the spice mixture into the saucepan, add the tomato purée and stir. (Stand well back as you stir. Some of the seeds may pop out of the pan.) Now add the potatoes and cauliflower and cook for about three minutes, stirring continuously. If the mixture starts to burn, turn the heat down.

7. Add 120 ml water to the saucepan, turn up the heat and bring the water to the boil.

8. Turn the heat down and leave your curry to simmer gently for about 15 minutes. Stir occasionally.

9. Meanwhile, chop the coriander or parsley into tiny pieces.

10. When your curry is cooked, spoon it into the serving dish, sprinkle the chopped coriander or parsley on top, and serve it hot.

Life in India

Over 1 billion people live in India, more than in any other country apart from China. And the population is still growing. Despite the fact that many people are very poor, Indian life is full of colour and bustle, a real mixture of modern and traditional.

WHERE PEOPLE LIVE

More than two-thirds of Indian people live in the thousands of villages dotted all over India. Most people work on the land. They do not own large farms; many own or rent small pieces of land. Here they grow food for their families, with perhaps a bit extra to sell at market. It is a hard life. People live in simple houses, sometimes built around open-air courtyards. Each village also has a well and a temple or mosque.

Some people leave their villages and travel to the big cities in search of work. Some get jobs as household servants, hotel workers or rickshaw drivers. But many return empty-handed. Indian cities are very overcrowded. Many people live in slums on the outskirts of the city. Some cannot even afford to do this. They sleep on the pavement. There are also gangs of beggars, trying to scrape together enough money to live on. Wealthy people usually live in large blocks of flats. They have servants to cook, clean and keep house for them.

EXTENDED FAMILIES

If you lived in India, you'd probably have not only your parents, but your grandparents, aunts, uncles and cousins living with you. When an Indian girl gets married, she leaves her family and goes to live with her husband's family. Indian weddings are very grand affairs, lasting for several days. The bride wears a special, embroidered sari with beautiful jewellery and elaborate make-up.

GOING TO SCHOOL

Indian children are supposed to go to school from the ages of 6 to 14. But children from poor families often leave school early or never go at all. Their families need them to work and earn some money. Apart from ordinary schools, there are also religious schools and schools which teach practical skills such as farming or health care. Village schools are often held in the open air. The children sit on the ground and write on slates, or in the sandy soil.

INDIAN NEWS

Each year, over 35,000 newspapers and magazines are published in India. They are printed in many different languages. The most famous English-language newspapers are the *Statesman* and the *Times of India*. Many of the most popular glossy magazines are filled with stories and gossip about India's film stars.

Say it in Hindi		
गाँव	*gaamw*	village
शहर	*shahar*	city
घर	*ghar*	home; house
किसान	*kisaan*	farmer
परिवार	*pariwaar*	family
स्कूल	*skool*	school
अध्यापक	*adhyaapak*	teacher
कूआँ	*kuaam*	well
अखबार	*akbaar*	newspaper
किताब	*kitaab*	book

Putting on a Sari

1. Put on the petticoat and T-shirt. Wrap one end of the material around your waist to form half a skirt and tuck the edge into the waistband of your petticoat.

2. Pick up the other end of the material and pull it around the back of your waist . . .

YOU WILL NEED:

A SHORT SLEEVED T-SHIRT

A LONG PETTICOAT

A LENGTH OF MATERIAL ABOUT 4 X 1 METRE

3. . . . across your chest . . .

4. . . . and up over your shoulder. The loose end of the material should drape down your back to your knees.

5. Hold out the middle section of the material, as shown.

6. Fold the loose material like a fan until the "skirt" fits you. Tuck the tops of the folds into your petticoat's waistband. The folds should face the same way as the shoulder covered by the loose end of your sari.

7. Check that the hem at the bottom of your sari is even, and straighten the material draped over your shoulder.

Sport and Leisure

Indian people work hard but they also find time to enjoy themselves. Playing and watching cricket, going to the cinema and story-telling are popular Indian pastimes.

SPORT

Many Indians are cricket mad. The national team are closely followed and their performances, good and bad, much discussed! Kite-flying, *kabbadi* (see below), polo and chess are all traditional Indian sports.

INDIAN DANCE

Kathakali is an ancient, traditional style of Indian dance from South India. Only men are allowed to dance the main roles. They wear elaborate masks and costumes, with brightly painted faces. They dance stories from Indian myths and legends.

FILM-GOING

Which city do you think makes the most feature films? Hollywood? Wrong! The answer is Mumbai (Bombay). Studios there make about 800 action-packed feature films each year. There are hundreds of cinemas all over India, and travelling cinema vans which visit remote villages. And just to show how popular Indian films are, some 100 million tickets are sold every week!

KABBADDI

This popular Indian game is a bit like team wrestling. One player has to run into the other team's territory, touch as many of his or her opponents as possible, and then race back to his or her own side without being captured by those that were touched. Now comes the tricky part. All of this has to be done in just one breath! If the player manages to make it back to base in a single breath, all those that were touched are out. To show that the player hasn't taken a sneaky second breath, he or she has to keep repeating the word "kabbaddi".

Say it in Hindi

खेल   *khayl* – game, sport

शतरंज   *shatranj* – chess

पतंग   *patang* – kite

नाच   *naach* – dance

संगीत   *sangeet* – music

बाजा   *baajaa* – musical instrument

Indian Religions

Religion plays an important part in the lives of Indian people. Many different religions are followed. People may be Hindus, Muslims, Sikhs, Jains, Buddhists or Christians. The main religion of India is Hinduism.

HINDUISM

About 8 out of 10 Indians are Hindus. They believe in a supreme being, called Brahman. This being is represented by three main gods – Brahma (the creator), Vishnu (the preserver) and Shiva (the destroyer). But there are thousands of other minor gods and goddesses. They include the elephant-headed god, Ganesh, and the monkey god, Hanuman. Hindus believe that when they die they are born again. Their aim is to break free of this cycle of birth and rebirth. If you lead a good life, you are more likely to do this than if you are bad.

Hindus worship the gods in many different ways. Some people visit a temple and take offerings of flowers and sweets. Others have small shrines at home where the family worships. Some Hindus don't worship at all – it's not compulsory!

Varanasi on the River Ganges is the holiest city for Hindus. They travel there from all over India to bathe in the river. This is believed to help them break free of the cycle of rebirth.

THE CASTE SYSTEM

Hindu society is traditionally divided into four castes (or classes). These were based on the types of jobs people did long ago. The highest caste is that of the *Brahmins* or priests. Next come the *Kshatriyas*, the soldiers and noblemen. They are followed by the *Vaishyas*, the merchants and traders, and the *Shudras*, the craftsmen and servants. People normally marry others of the same caste but that is not always the case today.

FOLLOWERS OF ISLAM

About a tenth of Indians are Muslims who follow the religion of Islam. They worship in buildings called mosques (see right) and have to pray every day. Muslims believe in one God, called Allah, and in his prophet, Muhammad. India's neighbours, Pakistan and Bangladesh, are both mainly Muslim countries.

OTHER FAITHS

There are also about 20 million Christians, 18 million Sikhs, 6 million Buddhists and 4 million Jains in India. The Sikh religion was founded in the Punjab in the 15th century by Guru Nanak. Sikhs worship in temples, called gurdwaras. Their most important temple is the Golden Temple in Amritsar (see page 7). The Jain and Buddhist religions were both founded in about 500 BC. One of the most sacred Buddhist sites is Sarnath in North India (see left). This is where the Buddha preached his first sermon.

Say it in Hindi

मसजिद *masjid* – mosque

साधू *saadhu* – Hindu holy man

मंदिर *mandeer* – temple

देवता *dayvtaa* – god, deity

पूजा *poojaa* – Hindu worship/prayers

बन्दर *bandar* – monkey

हाथी *haatee* – elephant

Festivals

There are hundreds of festivals and holidays in India. Many are religious holy days. Some are local village celebrations; others involve the whole country. There are also national holidays such as Republic Day on 26 January.

DIWALI

Diwali is one of the most important Hindu festivals. It takes place in late October or early November. Diwali is dedicated to the goddess of wealth and fortune, Lakshmi. It is celebrated with lights and fireworks, and with gifts of new clothes and silver jewellery.

HOLI

Holi is the Hindu festival which marks the beginning of spring, in March or April. On the night before Holi, people burn models of the witch, Holika, on bonfires. On the day of Holi itself, they drench each other with coloured water – it's great fun but very messy. The evening is spent visiting relatives with gifts of sweets and good wishes

RAMADAN

Ramadan is the most important festival in the Muslim year. It is a holy month of fasting. You are not allowed to eat or drink from dawn to dusk. Id-ul-Fitr is the day marking the end of Ramadan and the welcome end of the month's fasting.

REPUBLIC DAY

India officially became a republic on 26 January 1950. The 26 January is celebrated each year as the national day. There is a grand military parade down Raj Path in the capital, New Delhi, complete with beautifully decorated, ceremonial elephants.

Say it in Hindi

कपड़े	*kapray* – clothes
छुट्टी	*chuttee* – holiday
मेला	*maylaa* – festival, fair
राजधानी	*raajdhaanee* – capital city
आग	*aag* – fire
साल	*saal* – year

Shadow Shows

Shadow puppets are flat figures which are held against the back of a screen and lit from behind. The light throws shadows from the puppets onto the screen. The audience, sitting in front of the screen, watches the shadows move as the puppets are operated from behind by rods.

India has an ancient tradition of shadow theatre, which still survives in some parts of the country. Like the shadow shows of long ago, most modern shadow plays in India are based on stories about a hero called Rama, one of the forms of the god Vishnu. Once a year, a shadow play about Rama's victory over a 10-headed demon called Ravanna is performed in Kerala, in honour of the goddess Bhadrakali.

According to legend, Bhadrakali couldn't watch Rama's struggle with the evil Ravanna because she was busy fighting a battle of her own. So a shadow puppet version of the struggle was created for her to watch instead.

When this play is performed in front of Bhadraki temples today, the performances last between one and three weeks.

To stage your own shadow show . . .

YOU WILL NEED:

100 WATT READING LAMP OR PROJECTION LIGHT

THUMB TACKS

AN OLD WHITE COTTON SHEET

MIRROR

2 'G' CLAMPS

THIN DARK CARD

STICKY TAPE

2 LENGTHS OF BALSA WOOD, 75 x 2·5 x 2·5 cm

2 LENGTHS OF BALSA WOOD, 30 x 2·5 x 2·5 cm

SCISSORS

BALSA WOOD GLUE

A HOLE PUNCH OR THICK NEEDLE

CRAFT KNIFE

COLOURED CELLOPHANE SWEET WRAPPERS

THIN GARDEN RODS

The wood measurements given here will make a shadow theatre 75 cm long and 32 cm high. You can, of course, make your shadow theatre and puppets any size you like as long as they are easy to see at a distance.

To make the shadow screen

1. Glue the lengths of balsa wood together to make a frame.

19

2. Cut out a piece of sheet, big enough to cover one side of your frame. Gently stretch the material over the frame and pin it on opposite sides with the thumb tacks. Stretch the material again and pin the two remaining sides.

3. Cover a high table with a tablecloth and fix your screen to it with the "G" clamps. The tablecloth will hide your body when you sit behind the screen. Your audience will sit on the other side of the screen to watch the play.

4. Ask an adult to help you set up the reading lamp behind your screen. The lamp should be higher than your head will be when you are sitting down, to stop your shadow from appearing on the screen.

To make the shadow puppets

Some Indian shadow puppets are two metres tall!

5. Draw the outline of a puppet on the card and cut it out.

6. Using the hole punch or needle, make slits and holes in your puppet to suggest eyes, costume and jewellery. When the light shines on these holes, they will show through as white. If you want to create colour effects, stick some coloured cellophane over the cuts.

7. Tape a garden rod to the back of your puppet with sticky tape so that you can move the puppet from below. Then make more puppets in the same way.

8. Stand a mirror in front of your screen as shown, and turn on the reading lamp. Now try pressing your puppets against the screen and then holding them further away. If you look in the mirror as you do this, you'll be able to see the different types of shadows you are making.

Indian shadow puppets are usually made from leather. Some have no joints and cast black and white shadows onto the screen. Others have moveable arms and legs and cast coloured shadows instead. The leather used to make coloured shadow puppets is scraped very thin and is dyed different colours.

9. When you've seen what your puppets' shadows can do, invent a play for them. Cut out some card scenery and wedge it between the back of your screen and the frame. (Don't forget to remove the mirror when you stage your play in front of an audience.)

Getting About

Indian people love to travel. They make long journeys to visit relatives and attend weddings, and pilgrimages to special temples and other sacred places. The big cities are always full of noise and traffic, as people travel to work and to school. Many traffic jams are caused by cows wandering into the road. Because they are sacred, you are not supposed to hurry them on!

RAIL JOURNEYS

India has one of the biggest railway systems in the world. And one of the best used! The railways carry some 4.8 billion passengers a year. Many of the locomotives are still powered by steam.

BY BUS

Buses and coaches are usually packed so full, people have to sit on the roof or hang on to the sides. Many of the tourist coaches have air conditioning in them.

RICKSHAW POWER

Rickshaws can nip easily in and out of even the busiest traffic. Today they are pulled along by people riding cycles or motor scooters. They used to be pulled along by hand.

INDIAN AIRLINES

Air India is the national airline of India and there are four international airports in Delhi, Mumbai, Calcutta and Chennai. Indian Airlines carries passengers on internal flights. There is also a private internal airline, Vayur.

CAMEL RIDING

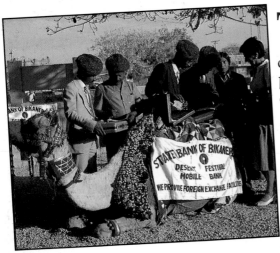

The best way to travel in the desert is on the back of a camel. Take a cushion – it can be a bumpy ride. In some places camels are used to bring banking services to people.

Say it in Hindi

ऊँट   *oomt* – camel

गाड़ी   *gaaree* – car

डाकिया   *daakiyaa* – postman

रिक्सा   *rikshaa* – rickshaw

स्टेशन   *stayshun* – station

Arts and Crafts

Indian arts and handicrafts are famous throughout the world. They include paintings, wooden carvings, brasswork and silver work, and fabulous fabrics and fabric designs. Many of these goods are made by small family-run businesses, based in the villages. The skills are passed down from one generation to the next.

MUGHAL MINIATURES

Miniature painting became popular from about the 14th century and was used to decorate religious works. The most beautiful paintings were done by artists working for the Rajput princes of Rajasthan. This style of painting flourished in the Mughal court in the 16th and 17th centuries.

FABRIC DESIGN

India is one of the world's top producers of cotton and silk. Each region of India has a special way of dyeing and decorating the cloth. In Varanasi, gold and silver thread are woven into silk. Saris made from this material are often worn at weddings.

The speciality of Gujarat and Rajasthan is mirror work. Tiny mirrors are sewn into cotton cloth for decoration. Tie dye designs are also very popular (see pages 25–7).

23

PAPIER MÂCHÉ AND CARPETS

Kashmir is famous for its papier mâché work. You can buy boxes, letter racks, cups, trays, anything you fancy. Kashmir is also where the best Indian carpets are made. They are woven from wool or silk, and are very expensive.

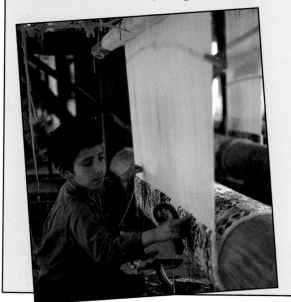

WOOD CARVING

Statues of the Hindu gods and goddesses are often carved from sandalwood, which has a pleasant, natural smell. The craftsmen carve very fine details onto the wood – it takes a steady hand.

JEWELS OF INDIA

Indian women like to wear lots of jewellery – bangles, earrings, necklaces, ankle chains and so on. Jewellery is usually made from gold or silver, with precious or semi-precious stones. Extra-special jewellery is worn for weddings.

Say it in Hindi

तस्वीर	*tasweer* – picture
चित्र	*chitra* – picture
दरज़ी	*darzee* – tailor
साड़ी	*saaree* – sari
सन्दूक	*sandook* – box
लकड़ी	*lakree* – wood
जवाहर	*jawaahar* – jewel

Tie and Dye

Tie and dye is one of the easiest ways of turning a boring white fabric into a jazzy patterned one. Parts of the fabric are knotted or tied so that when the whole piece of cloth is dyed, the tied parts remain the colour of the fabric whilst the rest becomes the colour of the dye. This produces an unusual pattern when the ties are undone.

YOU WILL NEED:

3-8 LARGE WHITE COTTON HANDKERCHIEFS, WHICH HAVE BEEN WASHED

OLD NEWSPAPER

HOT TAP WATER

4 TABLESPOONS OF SALT

OLD SPOON

WASHING POWDER

LARGE PLASTIC BUCKET OR BOWL

RUBBER GLOVES

1 TABLESPOON OF WASHING SODA

SHARP KNIFE

MEASURING JUG

APRON

ELASTIC BANDS

1 SMALL TIN OF DYLON COLD WATER DYE

FINE STRING

MARBLES

(IF YOU WANT TO CREATE MULTI-COLOURED PATTERNS, YOU WILL NEED A SECOND TIN OF DYE IN ANOTHER COLOUR, AND TWICE AS MUCH SALT AND WASHING SODA.)

1. To create a spotted pattern, twist some marbles into one of the handkerchiefs and hold them in place with the elastic bands. Twist and tie as tightly as you can to stop the dye from seeping into the tied parts of the cloth.

2. To create stripes, pleat the second handkerchief lengthwise and tie it tightly at intervals.

3. Fold, knot or bind the remaining handkerchief/s in other ways to create different patterns. Remember that the tied parts will resist the dye, and so form your pattern.

4. Pour enough cold water into the bucket or bowl to cover all the handkerchiefs.

5. Spread some newspaper over any surfaces that might get splashed with dye. Then put on the rubber gloves and apron and carefully pierce a large hole in the tin of dye.

6. Dissolve the dye in 1/2 litre of hot water and pour the solution into the bucket.

7. Put the soda and salt into the jug and dissolve them in 1/2 litre of hot water.

8. Pour the soda and salt solution into the bucket and stir well.

9. Wet the handkerchiefs, put them into the bucket and stir continually for 10 minutes. Then stir at intervals for 50 minutes, making sure that you keep the handkerchiefs submerged. (If you find it hard to tie them tightly, try leaving the handkerchiefs in the dye for only 30 minutes.)

10. Remove the handkerchiefs from the bucket and rinse them under the cold tap until the water runs clear. Then wash them in hot water and washing powder and rinse well.

11. Use pointed scissors to cut off the bindings and dry the handkerchiefs away from sunlight and direct heat.

You'll need to wash the handkerchiefs separately for the first few washes to get rid of any unfixed dye.

To create multi-coloured patterns, you can add more bindings after step 10, and then go back to step 5 and dye your handkerchiefs a different colour. Or you can cut your first bindings after step 10 and tie new ones in different places before dyeing them with a second colour.

This pattern was produced by twisting marbles into the fabric, dyeing it red, removing the marbles, and re-dyeing the fabric in yellow.

To create this pattern, the fabric was pleated and tied as shown in step 2, and dyed red. The outer bindings were then undone and the whole piece was re-dyed in yellow.

This pattern was produced by binding the centre of the fabric and dyeing the whole piece yellow. Once dry, this binding was undone and the centre of the fabric was pinched up and held in place by an elastic band. The four corners of the fabric were then tied with elastic bands and the whole piece was dyed green.

Indian History

India is an ancient country, with a long and colourful history. It has attracted explorers and traders for centuries, many of whom stayed to rule the country. Here are some of the very many key events and characters in Indian history.

THE MUGHAL EMPIRE

In the 16th century, India was conquered by the Mughals, a group of Muslims who invaded from the north west. They ruled over a huge empire, and were responsible for many of India's finest paintings, buildings and gardens. The Mughals had their capital at Agra. Their greatest emperor, Akbar, built a new city for himself to the west of Agra. It was called Fatehpur Sikri. But the city was abandoned after just 14 years because of problems with its water supply.

THE INDUS VALLEY CIVILISATION

The first great civilisation in India flourished along the banks of the River Indus in 2,500 BC. (This area is now part of Pakistan). It had highly organised cities at Mohenjo Daro and Harappa. Each house had a bathroom and the cities had very good drainage systems. Lots of artefacts have been dug up on the sites of the cities. Among them are hundreds of carved stone seals which were used to stamp a merchant's mark on his goods.

ASHOKA MAURYA

King Ashoka Maurya came to the throne in 269 BC and was one of India's greatest rulers. His empire covered most of India. In 260 BC, Ashoka decided to become a Buddhist and follow the Buddha's belief in peace and non-violence. Ashoka had just waged a successful but bloody war and was filled with remorse for all the people his troops had killed. Ashoka built the lion capital which is now India's national emblem (see page 5).

THE BRITISH RAJ

By 1756, Mughal power was in decline and the British were set to take control of India. They had come to India to trade but had gradually strengthened their power and position. In 1876, Queen Victoria was proclaimed Empress of India. India remained part of the British Empire until its independence in 1947.

MAHATMA GANDHI

Mohandas Gandhi was one of the most important campaigners for India's independence. He became known as "Mahatma" which means "great soul". He believed in non-violent, passive resistance. This meant that people marched in protest against the British but were asked not to use violence even if they were attacked.

INDIAN INDEPENDENCE

At the end of the 19th century, a group of young, educated Indians founded the Indian National Congress. Its aim was to campaign for a greater say for Indians in how they ran their country. The British agreed to many of their requests but also broke their promises. The "Quit India" campaign grew stronger after World War II, and in 1947 the last Viceroy of India, Lord Mountbatten, presided over India's independence. Jawaharlal Nehru became the country's first prime minister.

Say it in Hindi

देश *daysh* – country

शेर *sher* – lion

लड़ाई *laraaee* – war

राजा *raajaa* – king

राजनीति *raajneeti* – politics

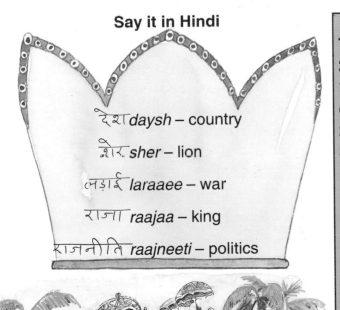

TIME BAND

2,500 BC Indus Valley Civilisation

1,500 BC The Aryans begin to invade

c563 BC Birth of the Buddha

269–231 BC Reign of King Ashoka

320 AD Founding of the Gupta Empire in India

1001 Muslim raids in the north-west

1498 Vasco Da Gama from Portugal sails to India, opening up a trade route from Europe

1526 The Mughal Empire begins

1784 The British take control of India

1857 The First War of Independence (Indian Mutiny)

1876 Queen Victoria is proclaimed Empress of India

1885 The Indian National Congress is founded

1947 India gains independence but is divided into Hindu India and Muslim Pakistan

1950 India becomes a republic

Picture Pairs

Play Picture Pairs and see how many of the Indian words in this book you actually remember! The instructions given here are for two to four players, but as your Indian vocabulary increases, you might like to make more cards and include more players.

YOU WILL NEED:

OLD MAGAZINES

WRAPPING PAPER

METAL RULER

GLUE

SCISSORS

STIFF PAPER

THICK CARD

CUTTING BOARD

PAINTS OR CRAYONS

PENCIL

CRAFT KNIFE

To make the cards

1. Draw 50 rectangles of the same size onto the card and carefully cut them out using the craft knife.

2. Draw another 50 rectangles onto the wrapping paper and cut them out too. These rectangles should be about 2 cm longer and wider than the card ones.

3. Cut the the corners of the paper rectangles as shown and glue them onto your cards.

4. Draw 25 rectangles, slightly smaller than your cards onto the stiff paper and cut them out.

5. Choose 25 Indian words from this book and write them down with their English translations. (Keep this list beside you as you play the game.)

30

6. Look through the magazines and cut out any photographs which illustrate the words you have chosen. If you can't find suitable pictures, cut out some more rectangles from stiff paper and paint pictures of your words on them.

जवाहर (Jawaahar)

कपड़े (kapray)

हाथी (haatee)

सब्ज़ी (sabzee)

सूरज (sooraj)

7. Stick each photograph or picture onto the front of one of your cards. Glue the stiff paper rectangles onto the rest of the pack and write a Indian word from your list on each one.

To play the game
The object of Picture Pairs is to collect pairs of cards made up of words and their matching picture.

Each player starts the game with seven cards. The rest of the pack is placed face down on the table. If you have any pairs, put them on the table in front of you.

Then ask one of the other players if he/she has a card that you need to make a pair. If that player has the card requested, he/she must hand it over and you win the pair and have another turn. If he/she does not have the card, you take a card from the pack in the middle and the turn passes to the next person.

All word cards must be translated into English. If you cannot remember the translation of a Hindi word, look it up and miss your next go.

The player who pairs all his/her cards first is the winner.

31

Index

Additional photographs:
DAS: 5, 13, 18, 28, cover.
Hulton Deutsch: 29. Hutchison:
cover, 9, 12, 15, 22, 23. Image:
4. Robert Harding: cover, 6, 8,
16, 17, 23, 24, 28. Werner
Foreman Archive: 6, 23. Zefa:
cover, 6, 7, 12, 15, 16, 24.